In Dad We Trust

The Bad Puppy's Guide to Life

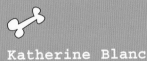

Katherine Blanc

SOURCEBOOKS HYSTERIA™
AN IMPRINT OF SOURCEBOOKS, INC.®
NAPERVILLE, ILLINOIS

Published by Sourcebooks, Inc.
P.O. Box 4410, Naperville, Illinois 60567-4410
(630) 961-3900
FAX: (630) 961-2168
www.sourcebooks.com

ISBN 1-4022-0340-3

Printed and bound in China
SNP   10 9 8 7 6 5 4 3 2 1

Dedicated to my father,
C.W. "Bill" Hushaw

Attention All Puppies:

- Are you getting what you want from life?
- Are you feeling powerless in your human home?
- Are you wishing you were having more fun?
- Are you getting the attention you crave?

Now...
The Bad Puppy's Guide to Life has the answers.
The Bad Puppy way helps you deal effectively with humans and get more out of life. Demonstrations and time-tested tips put you back in control of your world without jeopardizing the many benefits of domestication.

Don't let opportunity pass you by!
Read **The Bad Puppy's Guide to Life**

The Human Element

When you follow the way of the
Bad Puppy, you can be naughty
& nice at the same time.

A Bad Puppy is skilled in
the art of being adorable.

Always keep the humans guessing.

If at first you don't succeed,
bark, bark, bark again.

An empty lap is fair game.

Who's the boss?

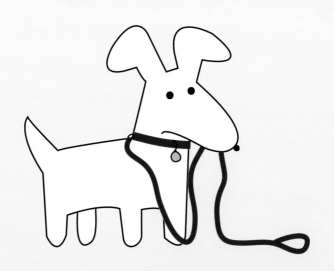

Command:

"Come"....................................

"Sit"....................................

"Stay"....................................

"Down"....................................

"Heel"....................................

"No!"....................................

Interpretation:

..............................."Run away"

..............................."Jump"

..............................."Let's go"

..............................."Play dumb"

..............................."Get the kitty"

..............................."Okay!!"

A proper response to
unpleasant requests.

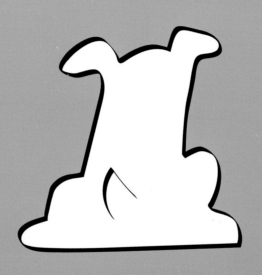

Revenge is sweet.

It's not the size, it's the attitude.

You can never have too many cookies.

Puppy Fantasy
#1

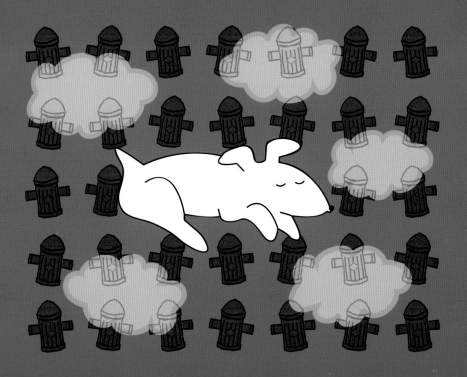

PUPPY
AT
PLAY

A Bad Puppy thrives on opportunity.

So many choices...

Puppy Fantasy
#2

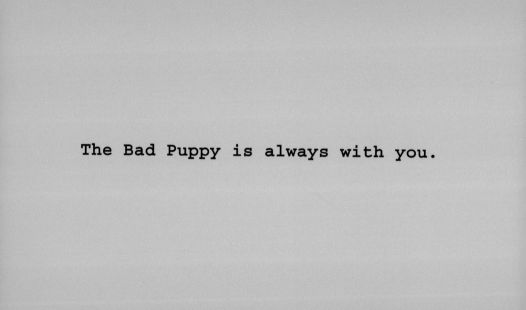

The Bad Puppy is always with you.

Why beg when you can steal?

If it smells bad, roll in it.

Persistence pays off.

The ideal snack?
An expensive leather shoe.

(preferably Italian)

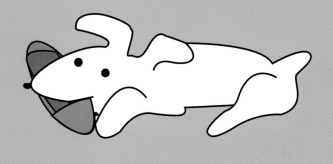

Enjoy the good life.

Explore your creative side.

Get plenty of exercise.

Refresh yourself.

Duh!

Sometimes it's best to lay low.

It happens.

The Bad Puppy wishes to thank
the following humans:

Noel Blanc, for his encouragement, love,
and praise (which every puppy craves),

Deborah Werksman, "Editor Extraordinaire,"
and the entire staff at Sourcebooks, Inc.

...plus one puppy: Elvis, the psychic poodle
and inspiration for this book.